The Happy Reader™

READING COMPREHENSION WORKBOOK

Grade 5

The Happy Reader™

READING COMPREHENSION WORKBOOK

Writing & Reasoning

Grade 5

Happy Readers are Lifelong Learners

STARRY FIELD PRESS

ISBN: 979-8-9949002-5-3
Printed in *the United States of America*

Publisher:
Starry Field Press
1401 21st St
Sacramento, CA 95811
www.starryfieldpress.com

Contact:
info@starryfieldpress.com

ABOUT THE PUBLISHER

Starry Field Press is a scholarly independent publishing house that allows educators, leaders, and clinicians to share their expertise beyond the academic audience. The Press believes that *Scholarship is a Field of Stars*. Through wide publication, talented professionals can shine far past their chosen fields.

The Press supports five celestial-inspired imprints: Via Scholastica (for Educators), Via Ducis (for Leaders), Via Medici (for Clinicians), Via Classica (for Nostalgics) and Via Risus (for Young Readers). *The Happy Reader* ™ *Series* is published under the imprint Via Risus (from Latin *risus*, laughter) which supports young readers to gain skills that will help them to be life-long learners.

For more information about Starry Field Press, please visit:

starryfieldpress.com

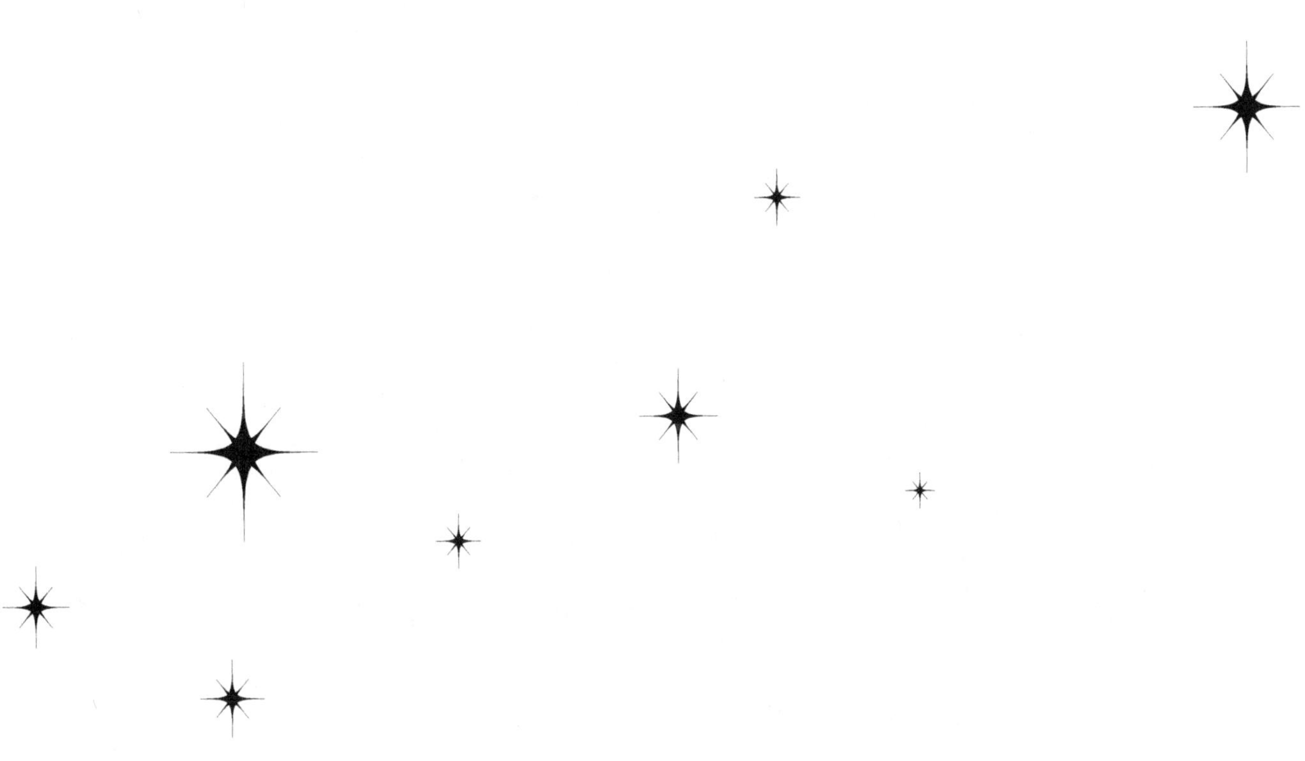

CONTENTS

Dear Reader,

Welcome to The Happy Reader!

This workbook is for you. You will read books and think deeply about ideas, messages, and themes. You will compare texts, consider author assumptions, and explain your thinking with evidence. You will write, talk, and share your ideas thoughtfully.

There are no trick questions. There are no one-right answers. Your reasoning and ideas are important.

Sometimes you will notice multiple themes. Sometimes you will question why authors make choices. Sometimes your thinking may change as you reflect. That is what skilled readers do.

Take your time. Think critically. Enjoy the journey of thinking carefully about books.

THE HAPPY READER WOOKBOOK

Dear Parents, Caregivers, Teachers, and Helpers,

Welcome to The Happy Reader series!

These workbooks focus on synthesis, evaluation, and critical thinking. He or she will compare texts, evaluate author assumptions, and articulate ideas with evidence. This work builds habits of lifelong reading, critical reasoning, and reflective thinking.

This series was created for families, educators, and learning communities who value meaning, reasoning, and the joy of reading. It is designed for children performing in the upper ranges of reading ability, while remaining flexible for all learners.

Each workbook is used after a child reads a book of his or her choosing, with space for 30 books. This allows roughly one book per week during the school year or a strong summer reading program. The goal is to integrate naturally into classrooms, home routines, libraries, and tutoring sessions.

Your role is to ask analytical questions, encourage multiple forms of evidence, and support reflection, without providing answers. Invite him or her to consider author choices, compare texts, and justify reasoning. This reflects Critical Literacy and Evidence-Based Thinking, as well as the Gradual Release of Responsibility, helping your child take ownership of independent, thoughtful analysis.

GRADE 5

Introduction to the Happy Reader Series

The Happy Reader is a Kindergarten through Grade 5 reading comprehension curriculum built around thoughtful reading. The focus is meaning, reasoning, and the joy of reading.

Children learn to understand stories, explain ideas, and reflect on their own thinking. As they grow, they learn to support ideas with evidence, consider different perspectives, and write with clarity and care.

The curriculum is customizable. Any appropriate book may be used. This flexibility allows children to read widely while engaging in consistent intellectual routines. The structure remains familiar across grades. The thinking grows more complex each year. This balance supports confidence without limiting challenge.

How Learning Progresses

Reading development in *The Happy Reader* follows a clear progression.

Kindergarten focuses on story sense.
Children identify characters and settings, retell events, express feelings, and connect stories to their own lives.

Grade 1 introduces structure.
Children explore beginning, middle, and end, problem and solution, and simple explanations.

Grade 2 emphasizes cause and change.
Children consider motivation, use textual clues, and explain ideas using "because."

Grade 3 centers on inference and theme.
Children distinguish main ideas from details, support thinking with evidence, and reflect on their learning.

Grade 4 develops analysis and perspective.
Children examine character growth, point of view, symbolism, and author choices.

Grade 5 brings synthesis and argument.
Children compare texts, evaluate ideas, identify assumptions, and write thoughtful critiques.

THE HAPPY READER WOOKBOOK

Workbook Structure

Each workbook follows a predictable and supportive routine. Every page includes:
- Book information
- Core comprehension tasks
- Evidence-based prompts
- Vocabulary exploration
- Optional challenge questions
- Reflection prompts

Reflection prompts

The visual structure of the workbook is consistent throughout. This design prompts the reader to anticipate the questions to be asked after reading a book. With practice, focus builds naturally and encourages ever more sophisticated understanding of the text. Facility and confidence encourage thinking about the story rather than only on the mechanics. Each of these new skills builds on another: thoughtful reflection of the text's meaning.

Before You Begin

At the start of the workbook:
- The child completes an initial self-assessment, reflecting on how he or she thinks about stories.
- An adult completes an initial observation, noting habits, confidence, and approach to reading.
- These assessments are about understanding learning patterns rather than correctness. They provide a baseline to notice growth.

Working Through the Workbook

The child reads 30 books, completing workbook pages after each one. Reflection is ongoing. Adults are encouraged to notice:
- How the child supports ideas with evidence
- Increasing clarity in writing
- How the child reflects on reading strategies

After Completion

At the end of the workbook:
- The child completes a post-workbook self-assessment
- The adult completes a post-workbook observation

These reflections help document growth in comprehension, reasoning, and participation across the reading cycle.

Pedagogical Framework

Grade 5 workbooks integrate *Critical Literacy*, *Gradual Release of Responsibility*, and *Synthesis and Argumentation* frameworks. Critical Literacy (Lewison, Leland, & Harste, 2002) encourages students to evaluate texts for purpose, perspective, and assumptions, moving beyond surface comprehension to analysis and critique. Gradual Release supports independence, shifting responsibility for thinking and writing from adults to students. Synthesis and Argumentation frameworks focus on integrating ideas across texts, comparing perspectives, and constructing evidence-based arguments.

Workbook tasks require children to analyze multiple themes, evaluate author messages, and support claims with textual evidence. Reflection prompts encourage self-assessment and reasoning about learning strategies. Adults observe and guide discussion but allow the child to take ownership, offering challenges rather than answers. This approach develops sophisticated thinking, reflective reading, and strong written expression, preparing students for middle school demands. By aligning Critical Literacy with structured evidence-based exercises, the Grade 5 workbook fosters independent, analytical readers who can thoughtfully evaluate and argue ideas.

THE HAPPY READER WOOKBOOK

How to Use This Workbook

Choose a Book

Any age-appropriate fiction or nonfiction book may be used. Short chapter books with themes, multiple characters, or layered plots work best. Encourage choices that invite reflection books or picture books with clear storylines work well. Allow your child to choose a book that sparks curiosity.

Read Thoughtfully

Reading is independent. Encourage him or her to consider assumptions, themes, author purpose, and textual connections. Discussion may be used to clarify reasoning before writing.

Complete the Pages

Complete prompts in order or selectively. Encourage written sentences or short paragraphs that include textual evidence. Focus on inference, summarization, and supporting ideas.

Reflect Together

- "What patterns do you notice across the story or texts?"
- "How did your ideas change while reading?"
- "What evidence supports your conclusions?"

Look back at early pages. Notice development in analytical thinking, evidence use, and written clarity. Celebrate effort, independent reasoning, and reflective insights.

Advice for Adults

Support your child in reasoning and argumentation, not simply in giving answers. Encourage evidence-based analysis, synthesis of ideas, and thoughtful reflection. Emphasize skill development, curiosity, and independent thinking.

About the Reading Assessments

Purpose of the Assessments

This workbook includes two short assessments, one at the beginning of the reading sequence and one at the end. After your child has read or listened to 30 books, the second assessment helps you reflect on how comprehension has developed across time and practice.

Why There Are Two Assessments

Fifth-grade readers are preparing for the academic demands of middle school. Comprehension now involves analyzing ideas, recognizing author perspective, and sustaining attention across longer texts. The pre-reading assessment captures current reading behaviors. The post-reading assessment shows how those behaviors have evolved through consistent practice.

What the Assessments Include

Each assessment includes:
- A child self-assessment focused on awareness of understanding
- An adult observation centered on comprehension behaviors

Together, they offer complementary perspectives on growth.

How to Approach the Process

Treat the assessments as reflective conversations. Encourage thoughtful answers without correction. Base observations on patterns over time. A relaxed tone supports open reflection.

Pedagogical Framework

These assessments draw on *Strategic Reading Theory*, which views skilled reading as purposeful, flexible, and goal-directed. They also reflect *Disciplinary Literacy Frameworks*, which recognize that older readers engage with texts as sources of ideas, arguments, and evidence. The assessments support reflection on how readers approach meaning, not how fast they read.

THE HAPPY READER WOOKBOOK

Understanding Your Child's Pre-Reading Assessment

Purpose of the Pre-Reading Assessment

In Grade 5, comprehension includes synthesis, evaluation, and textual argumentation. This pre-reading assessment captures how your child interprets themes, identifies assumptions, and begins forming evidence-based opinions. It measures readiness for independent analysis and critique.

How to Complete the Assessment

- Read the questions together in a neutral tone.
- Respond based on what you normally observe during story time.
- Do not prompt, coach, or rehearse answers.

For the child self-assessment, explain that there are no right or wrong answers. Help him or her choose the response that feels most true.

How to Interpret Results

Focus on ability to identify themes, evaluate author assumptions, and use evidence. Responses highlight readiness for independent, analytical reading and writing. Differences in responses are normal and expected.

How This Helps Going Forward

The pre-assessment provides a benchmark for synthesis, argumentation, and reflective thinking. Comparing with the post-assessment will show growth in independent analysis, evidence-based reasoning, and critical reading skills. Adults can use these insights to support independent thinking, discussion, and writing throughout the workbook.

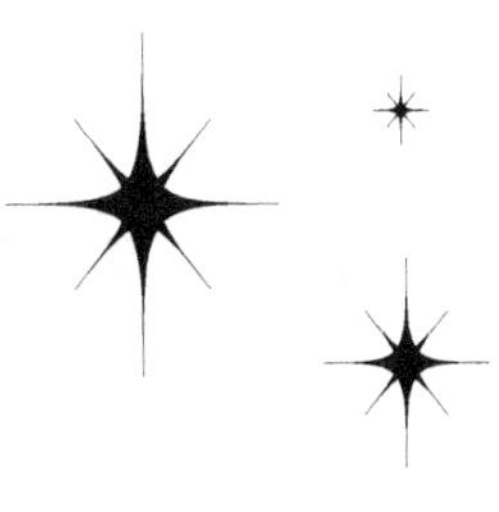

GRADE 5

Reader's Initial Reading Self-Assessment

Please choose how you feel about each sentence. Circle one.

1.   I evaluate characters, ideas, or choices.

Always (5)   Often (4)   Sometimes (3)   Rarely (2)   Not yet (1)

2.   I use evidence to support my ideas.

Always (5)   Often (4)   Sometimes (3)   Rarely (2)   Not yet (1)

3.   I reflect on how reading shapes my thinking.

Always (5)   Often (4)   Sometimes (3)   Rarely (2)   Not yet (1)

4.   I read with purpose and independence.

Always (5)   Often (4)   Sometimes (3)   Rarely (2)   Not yet (1)

5.   I look for patterns across a text.

Always (5)   Often (4)   Sometimes (3)   Rarely (2)   Not yet (1)

Total score (optional): ____ / 25

How do I connect the ideas or themes in a story with other stories I've read, or to my own thoughts?

____

____

____

____

____

THE HAPPY READER WOOKBOOK

Initial Reading Assessment by Parent, Caregiver, Teacher, or Helper

Adult Observation Inventory: Rate your observations of the reader.

1.　　Looks past the literal meaning in the text

　　　Consistently (5)　Often (4)　Sometimes (3)　Rarely (2)　Not observed (1)

2.　　Uses evidence or examples for statements

　　　Consistently (5)　Often (4)　Sometimes (3)　Rarely (2)　Not observed (1)

3.　　Searches for patterns in characters' behavior or story themes

　　　Consistently (5)　Often (4)　Sometimes (3)　Rarely (2)　Not observed (1)

4.　　Demonstrates sustained engagement in the understanding of the text

　　　Consistently (5)　Often (4)　Sometimes (3)　Rarely (2)　Not observed (1)

5.　　Demonstrates sustained engagement in the interpretation of the text

　　　Consistently (5)　Often (4)　Sometimes (3)　Rarely (2)　Not observed (1)

Total score (optional): ___ / 25

Qualitative assessment:

How does my child compare ideas or themes across different texts?________________

____

____

How does my child evaluate author assumptions or arguments?________________

____

____

How do I encourage critical thinking, reflection, and textual argumentation?____________

____

____

GRADE 5

Happy

Reading!

Interpret, Analyze, Argue   Book 1

Book Title: ____

Author: ____

Date:____

What Is the Author's Central Message?

Write a clear claim about what the author is trying to say about life, people, or the world

____

____

____

What Themes Appear in the Story?

List two themes and briefly explain each.

*Theme 1*____

____

Explain how this theme appears in the story _________________

____

____

____

*Theme 2*____

____

Explain how this theme appears in the story _________________

____

____

____

Character as an Idea

Choose one main character. What idea does this character represent?

____

____

____

Key Scene Analysis

Describe one scene that is especially important.

____

____

____

Why is this scene important to the story's meaning?

____

____

____

Evidence Matters

Write two pieces of evidence from the text that support your ideas.

*Evidence 1*____

____

____

*Evidence 2*____

____

____

Setting and Meaning

How does the setting influence the story's themes or conflicts?

____

____

____

____

Author's Perspective

What does the author seem to believe about people or the world?

____

____

____

____

____

Compare Texts

Think about another book you've read.

This book is similar to_______________________________

____

____

because both texts_______________________________

____

____

Author's Craft Deep Dive

Find one example of strong writing (imagery, symbolism, dialogue, or structure).

The author wrote____

____

____

____

This technique is effective because ____________________________

____

____

____

Critical Response

Do you agree with the author's message or perspective? Explain your thinking.

____

____

____

____

Metacognitive Reflection

What did this book help you understand better about yourself, others, or the world?

____

____

____

____

Interpret, Analyze, Argue   Book 2

Book Title: ____

Author: ____

Date:____

What Is the Author's Central Message?

Write a clear claim about what the author is trying to say about life, people, or the world

____

____

____

What Themes Appear in the Story?

List two themes and briefly explain each.

*Theme 1*_______________________________________

____

Explain how this theme appears in the story ______________

____

____

____

*Theme 2*_______________________________________

____

Explain how this theme appears in the story ______________

____

____

____

THE HAPPY READER WOOKBOOK

Character as an Idea

Choose one main character. What idea does this character represent?

____

____

____

Key Scene Analysis

Describe one scene that is especially important.

____

____

____

Why is this scene important to the story's meaning?

____

____

____

Evidence Matters

Write two pieces of evidence from the text that support your ideas.

*Evidence 1*_______________________________________

____

____

____

*Evidence 2*_______________________________________

____

____

____

Setting and Meaning

How does the setting influence the story's themes or conflicts?

____

____

____

____

Author's Perspective

What does the author seem to believe about people or the world?

____

____

____

____

Compare Texts

Think about another book you've read.

This book is similar to_______________________________

____

____

because both texts_______________________________

____

____

Author's Craft Deep Dive

Find one example of strong writing (imagery, symbolism, dialogue, or structure).

The author wrote______________________________________

____

____

____

This technique is effective because ___________________

____

____

____

Critical Response

Do you agree with the author's message or perspective? Explain your thinking.

____

____

____

____

Metacognitive Reflection

What did this book help you understand better about yourself, others, or the world?

____

____

____

____

Interpret, Analyze, Argue   Book 3

Book Title: ____

Author: ____

Date:____

What Is the Author's Central Message?

Write a clear claim about what the author is trying to say about life, people, or the world

____

____

____

What Themes Appear in the Story?

List two themes and briefly explain each.

*Theme 1*____

____

Explain how this theme appears in the story ___________________

____

____

____

*Theme 2*____

____

Explain how this theme appears in the story ___________________

____

____

____

Character as an Idea

Choose one main character. What idea does this character represent?

____

____

____

Key Scene Analysis

Describe one scene that is especially important.

____

____

____

Why is this scene important to the story's meaning?

____

____

____

Evidence Matters

Write two pieces of evidence from the text that support your ideas.

*Evidence 1*_______________________________________

____

____

____

*Evidence 2*_______________________________________

____

____

____

GRADE 5

Setting and Meaning

How does the setting influence the story's themes or conflicts?

____

____

____

____

Author's Perspective

What does the author seem to believe about people or the world?

____

____

____

____

____

Compare Texts

Think about another book you've read.

This book is similar to_______________________________

____

____

because both texts_______________________________

____

____

Author's Craft Deep Dive

Find one example of strong writing (imagery, symbolism, dialogue, or structure).

The author wrote ____

____

____

____

This technique is effective because _______________________

____

____

____

Critical Response

Do you agree with the author's message or perspective? Explain your thinking.

____

____

____

____

Metacognitive Reflection

What did this book help you understand better about yourself, others, or the world?

____

____

____

____

Interpret, Analyze, Argue

Book 4

Book Title: ____

Author: ____

Date:____

What Is the Author's Central Message?

Write a clear claim about what the author is trying to say about life, people, or the world

____

____

____

What Themes Appear in the Story?

List two themes and briefly explain each.

*Theme 1*_____________________________________

____

Explain how this theme appears in the story ________________

____

____

____

*Theme 2*_____________________________________

____

Explain how this theme appears in the story ________________

____

____

____

Character as an Idea

Choose one main character. What idea does this character represent?

____

____

____

Key Scene Analysis

Describe one scene that is especially important.

____

____

____

Why is this scene important to the story's meaning?

____

____

____

Evidence Matters

Write two pieces of evidence from the text that support your ideas.

*Evidence 1*_______________________________________

____

____

*Evidence 2*_______________________________________

____

____

Setting and Meaning

How does the setting influence the story's themes or conflicts?

____

____

____

____

Author's Perspective

What does the author seem to believe about people or the world?

____

____

____

____

____

Compare Texts

Think about another book you've read.

This book is similar to_______________________________

____

____

because both texts_______________________________

____

____

Author's Craft Deep Dive

Find one example of strong writing (imagery, symbolism, dialogue, or structure).

The author wrote_______________________________________

____

____

____

This technique is effective because ____________________

____

____

____

Critical Response

Do you agree with the author's message or perspective? Explain your thinking.

____

____

____

____

Metacognitive Reflection

What did this book help you understand better about yourself, others, or the world?

____

____

____

____

Interpret, Analyze, Argue   Book 5

Book Title: ____

Author: ____

Date:____

What Is the Author's Central Message?

Write a clear claim about what the author is trying to say about life, people, or the world

____

____

____

What Themes Appear in the Story?

List two themes and briefly explain each.

*Theme 1*____

____

Explain how this theme appears in the story _______________________

____

____

____

*Theme 2*____

____

Explain how this theme appears in the story _______________________

____

____

____

Character as an Idea

Choose one main character. What idea does this character represent?

____

____

____

Key Scene Analysis

Describe one scene that is especially important.

____

____

____

Why is this scene important to the story's meaning?

____

____

____

Evidence Matters

Write two pieces of evidence from the text that support your ideas.

*Evidence 1*_______________________________________

____

____

*Evidence 2*_______________________________________

____

____

Setting and Meaning

How does the setting influence the story's themes or conflicts?

____

____

____

____

Author's Perspective

What does the author seem to believe about people or the world?

____

____

____

____

Compare Texts

Think about another book you've read.

This book is similar to_______________________________

____

____

because both texts_______________________________

____

____

Author's Craft Deep Dive

Find one example of strong writing (imagery, symbolism, dialogue, or structure).

The author wrote____

____

____

This technique is effective because _______________________________

____

____

Critical Response

Do you agree with the author's message or perspective? Explain your thinking.

____

____

____

____

Metacognitive Reflection

What did this book help you understand better about yourself, others, or the world?

____

____

____

____

Interpret, Analyze, Argue   Book 6

Book Title: ____

Author: ____

Date:____

What Is the Author's Central Message?

Write a clear claim about what the author is trying to say about life, people, or the world

____

____

____

What Themes Appear in the Story?

List two themes and briefly explain each.

*Theme 1*____

____

Explain how this theme appears in the story ____________________

____

____

____

*Theme 2*____

____

Explain how this theme appears in the story ____________________

____

____

____

Character as an Idea

Choose one main character. What idea does this character represent?

____

____

____

Key Scene Analysis

Describe one scene that is especially important.

____

____

____

Why is this scene important to the story's meaning?

____

____

____

Evidence Matters

Write two pieces of evidence from the text that support your ideas.

*Evidence 1*_______________________________________

____

____

____

*Evidence 2*_______________________________________

____

____

____

Setting and Meaning

How does the setting influence the story's themes or conflicts?

____

____

____

____

Author's Perspective

What does the author seem to believe about people or the world?

____

____

____

____

____

Compare Texts

Think about another book you've read.

This book is similar to_______________________________

____

____

because both texts_________________________________

____

____

Author's Craft Deep Dive

Find one example of strong writing (imagery, symbolism, dialogue, or structure).

The author wrote____

____

____

This technique is effective because _______________________

____

____

____

Critical Response

Do you agree with the author's message or perspective? Explain your thinking.

____

____

____

____

Metacognitive Reflection

What did this book help you understand better about yourself, others, or the world?

____

____

____

____

Interpret, Analyze, Argue   Book 7

Book Title: ____

Author: ____

Date:____

What Is the Author's Central Message?

Write a clear claim about what the author is trying to say about life, people, or the world

____

____

____

What Themes Appear in the Story?

List two themes and briefly explain each.

*Theme 1*____

____

Explain how this theme appears in the story _________________

____

____

____

*Theme 2*____

____

Explain how this theme appears in the story _________________

____

____

____

Character as an Idea

Choose one main character. What idea does this character represent?

____

____

____

Key Scene Analysis

Describe one scene that is especially important.

____

____

____

Why is this scene important to the story's meaning?

____

____

____

Evidence Matters

Write two pieces of evidence from the text that support your ideas.

*Evidence 1*____

____

____

*Evidence 2*____

____

____

Setting and Meaning

How does the setting influence the story's themes or conflicts?

____

____

____

____

Author's Perspective

What does the author seem to believe about people or the world?

____

____

____

____

Compare Texts

Think about another book you've read.

This book is similar to_______________________________

____

____

because both texts_______________________________

____

____

Author's Craft Deep Dive

Find one example of strong writing (imagery, symbolism, dialogue, or structure).

The author wrote_______________________________________

____

____

____

This technique is effective because _____________________

____

____

____

Critical Response

Do you agree with the author's message or perspective? Explain your thinking.

____

____

____

____

Metacognitive Reflection

What did this book help you understand better about yourself, others, or the world?

____

____

____

____

Interpret, Analyze, Argue   Book 8

Book Title: ____

Author: ____

Date:____

What Is the Author's Central Message?

Write a clear claim about what the author is trying to say about life, people, or the world

____

____

____

What Themes Appear in the Story?

List two themes and briefly explain each.

*Theme 1*____

____

Explain how this theme appears in the story _________________

____

____

____

*Theme 2*____

____

Explain how this theme appears in the story _________________

____

____

____

THE HAPPY READER WOOKBOOK

Character as an Idea

Choose one main character. What idea does this character represent?

____

____

____

Key Scene Analysis

Describe one scene that is especially important.

____

____

____

Why is this scene important to the story's meaning?

____

____

____

Evidence Matters

Write two pieces of evidence from the text that support your ideas.

*Evidence 1*_______________________________________

____

____

*Evidence 2*_______________________________________

____

____

____

Setting and Meaning

How does the setting influence the story's themes or conflicts?

____

____

____

Author's Perspective

What does the author seem to believe about people or the world?

____

____

____

____

Compare Texts

Think about another book you've read.

This book is similar to______________________________

____

____

because both texts______________________________

____

____

THE HAPPY READER WOOKBOOK

Author's Craft Deep Dive

Find one example of strong writing (imagery, symbolism, dialogue, or structure).

The author wrote____

____

____

____

This technique is effective because _________________________

____

____

____

Critical Response

Do you agree with the author's message or perspective? Explain your thinking.

____

____

____

____

Metacognitive Reflection

What did this book help you understand better about yourself, others, or the world?

____

____

____

____

Interpret, Analyze, Argue   Book 9

Book Title: ____

Author: ____

Date:____

What Is the Author's Central Message?

Write a clear claim about what the author is trying to say about life, people, or the world

____

____

____

What Themes Appear in the Story?

List two themes and briefly explain each.

*Theme 1*____

____

Explain how this theme appears in the story _______________

____

____

____

*Theme 2*____

____

Explain how this theme appears in the story _______________

____

____

____

THE HAPPY READER WOOKBOOK

Character as an Idea

Choose one main character. What idea does this character represent?

____

____

____

Key Scene Analysis

Describe one scene that is especially important.

____

____

____

Why is this scene important to the story's meaning?

____

____

____

Evidence Matters

Write two pieces of evidence from the text that support your ideas.

*Evidence 1*____________________________________

____

____

*Evidence 2*____________________________________

____

____

Setting and Meaning

How does the setting influence the story's themes or conflicts?

____

____

____

____

Author's Perspective

What does the author seem to believe about people or the world?

____

____

____

____

Compare Texts

Think about another book you've read.

This book is similar to______________________________

____

____

because both texts______________________________

____

____

Author's Craft Deep Dive

Find one example of strong writing (imagery, symbolism, dialogue, or structure).

The author wrote____

____

____

____

This technique is effective because _________________________

____

____

____

Critical Response

Do you agree with the author's message or perspective? Explain your thinking.

____

____

____

____

Metacognitive Reflection

What did this book help you understand better about yourself, others, or the world?

____

____

____

____

Interpret, Analyze, Argue   Book 10

Book Title: ____

Author: ____

Date:____

What Is the Author's Central Message?

Write a clear claim about what the author is trying to say about life, people, or the world

____

____

____

What Themes Appear in the Story?

List two themes and briefly explain each.

*Theme 1*_______________________________________

____

Explain how this theme appears in the story _______________

____

____

____

*Theme 2*_______________________________________

____

Explain how this theme appears in the story _______________

____

____

____

Character as an Idea

Choose one main character. What idea does this character represent?

____

____

____

Key Scene Analysis

Describe one scene that is especially important.

____

____

____

Why is this scene important to the story's meaning?

____

____

____

Evidence Matters

Write two pieces of evidence from the text that support your ideas.

*Evidence 1*_______________________________________

____

____

*Evidence 2*_______________________________________

____

____

Setting and Meaning

How does the setting influence the story's themes or conflicts?

____

____

____

____

Author's Perspective

What does the author seem to believe about people or the world?

____

____

____

____

____

Compare Texts

Think about another book you've read.

This book is similar to_________________________

____

____

because both texts_____________________________

____

____

Author's Craft Deep Dive

Find one example of strong writing (imagery, symbolism, dialogue, or structure).

The author wrote____

____

____

____

This technique is effective because ____________________________

____

____

____

Critical Response

Do you agree with the author's message or perspective? Explain your thinking.

____

____

____

____

Metacognitive Reflection

What did this book help you understand better about yourself, others, or the world?

____

____

____

____

Interpret, Analyze, Argue   Book 11

Book Title: ____

Author: ____

Date:____

What Is the Author's Central Message?

Write a clear claim about what the author is trying to say about life, people, or the world

____

____

____

What Themes Appear in the Story?

List two themes and briefly explain each.

*Theme 1*____

____

Explain how this theme appears in the story _____________________

____

____

____

*Theme 2*____

____

Explain how this theme appears in the story _____________________

____

____

____

Character as an Idea

Choose one main character. What idea does this character represent?

____

____

____

Key Scene Analysis

Describe one scene that is especially important.

____

____

____

Why is this scene important to the story's meaning?

____

____

____

Evidence Matters

Write two pieces of evidence from the text that support your ideas.

*Evidence 1*_________________________________

____

____

*Evidence 2*_________________________________

____

____

____

Setting and Meaning

How does the setting influence the story's themes or conflicts?

____

____

____

____

Author's Perspective

What does the author seem to believe about people or the world?

____

____

____

____

Compare Texts

Think about another book you've read.

This book is similar to___________________________

____

____

because both texts___________________________

____

____

Author's Craft Deep Dive

Find one example of strong writing (imagery, symbolism, dialogue, or structure).

The author wrote_______________________________

____

____

____

This technique is effective because ____________

____

____

____

Critical Response

Do you agree with the author's message or perspective? Explain your thinking.

____

____

____

____

Metacognitive Reflection

What did this book help you understand better about yourself, others, or the world?

____

____

____

____

Interpret, Analyze, Argue   Book 12

Book Title: ____

Author: ____

Date:____

What Is the Author's Central Message?

Write a clear claim about what the author is trying to say about life, people, or the world

____

____

____

What Themes Appear in the Story?

List two themes and briefly explain each.

*Theme 1*_______________________________________

____

Explain how this theme appears in the story _____________

____

____

____

*Theme 2*_______________________________________

____

Explain how this theme appears in the story _____________

____

____

____

THE HAPPY READER WOOKBOOK

Character as an Idea

Choose one main character. What idea does this character represent?

____

____

____

Key Scene Analysis

Describe one scene that is especially important.

____

____

____

Why is this scene important to the story's meaning?

____

____

____

Evidence Matters

Write two pieces of evidence from the text that support your ideas.

*Evidence 1*_______________________________________

____

____

*Evidence 2*_______________________________________

____

____

Setting and Meaning

How does the setting influence the story's themes or conflicts?

____

____

____

____

Author's Perspective

What does the author seem to believe about people or the world?

____

____

____

____

Compare Texts

Think about another book you've read.

This book is similar to_______________________________

____

because both texts_______________________________

____

Author's Craft Deep Dive

Find one example of strong writing (imagery, symbolism, dialogue, or structure).

The author wrote ____

____

____

____

This technique is effective because ___________________________

____

____

____

Critical Response

Do you agree with the author's message or perspective? Explain your thinking.

____

____

____

____

Metacognitive Reflection

What did this book help you understand better about yourself, others, or the world?

____

____

____

____

Interpret, Analyze, Argue   Book 13

Book Title: ____

Author: ____

Date:____

What Is the Author's Central Message?

Write a clear claim about what the author is trying to say about life, people, or the world

____

____

____

What Themes Appear in the Story?

List two themes and briefly explain each.

*Theme 1*____

____

Explain how this theme appears in the story _____________________

____

____

____

*Theme 2*____

____

Explain how this theme appears in the story _____________________

____

____

____

Character as an Idea

Choose one main character. What idea does this character represent?

____

____

____

Key Scene Analysis

Describe one scene that is especially important.

____

____

____

Why is this scene important to the story's meaning?

____

____

____

Evidence Matters

Write two pieces of evidence from the text that support your ideas.

*Evidence 1*_______________________________________

____

____

*Evidence 2*_______________________________________

____

____

GRADE 5

Setting and Meaning

How does the setting influence the story's themes or conflicts?

____

____

____

____

Author's Perspective

What does the author seem to believe about people or the world?

____

____

____

____

____

Compare Texts

Think about another book you've read.

This book is similar to_______________________________

____

____

because both texts_______________________________

____

____

THE HAPPY READER WOOKBOOK

Author's Craft Deep Dive

Find one example of strong writing (imagery, symbolism, dialogue, or structure).

The author wrote____

____

____

____

This technique is effective because _____________________________

____

____

____

Critical Response

Do you agree with the author's message or perspective? Explain your thinking.

____

____

____

____

Metacognitive Reflection

What did this book help you understand better about yourself, others, or the world?

____

____

____

____

Interpret, Analyze, Argue   Book 14

Book Title: ________________________________

Author: ___________________________________

Date:_____________________________________

What Is the Author's Central Message?

Write a clear claim about what the author is trying to say about life, people, or the world

____

____

____

What Themes Appear in the Story?

List two themes and briefly explain each.

*Theme 1*_______________________________

____

Explain how this theme appears in the story ____________

____

____

____

*Theme 2*_______________________________

____

Explain how this theme appears in the story ____________

____

____

____

Character as an Idea

Choose one main character. What idea does this character represent?

____

____

____

Key Scene Analysis

Describe one scene that is especially important.

____

____

____

Why is this scene important to the story's meaning?

____

____

____

Evidence Matters

Write two pieces of evidence from the text that support your ideas.

*Evidence 1*_______________________________________

____

____

*Evidence 2*_______________________________________

____

____

Setting and Meaning

How does the setting influence the story's themes or conflicts?

____

____

____

____

Author's Perspective

What does the author seem to believe about people or the world?

____

____

____

____

____

Compare Texts

Think about another book you've read.

This book is similar to_______________________________

____

____

because both texts_______________________________

____

____

Author's Craft Deep Dive

Find one example of strong writing (imagery, symbolism, dialogue, or structure).

The author wrote_______________________________________

____

____

This technique is effective because _______________

____

____

____

Critical Response

Do you agree with the author's message or perspective? Explain your thinking.

____

____

____

____

Metacognitive Reflection

What did this book help you understand better about yourself, others, or the world?

____

____

____

____

Interpret, Analyze, Argue   Book 15

Book Title: ____

Author: ____

Date:____

What Is the Author's Central Message?

Write a clear claim about what the author is trying to say about life, people, or the world

____

____

____

What Themes Appear in the Story?

List two themes and briefly explain each.

*Theme 1*____

____

Explain how this theme appears in the story _______________

____

____

____

*Theme 2*____

____

Explain how this theme appears in the story _______________

____

____

____

Character as an Idea

Choose one main character. What idea does this character represent?

____

____

____

Key Scene Analysis

Describe one scene that is especially important.

____

____

____

Why is this scene important to the story's meaning?

____

____

____

Evidence Matters

Write two pieces of evidence from the text that support your ideas.

*Evidence 1*_______________________________________

____

____

*Evidence 2*_______________________________________

____

____

Setting and Meaning

How does the setting influence the story's themes or conflicts?

____

____

____

____

Author's Perspective

What does the author seem to believe about people or the world?

____

____

____

____

____

Compare Texts

Think about another book you've read.

This book is similar to_______________________________

____

____

because both texts________________________________

____

____

THE HAPPY READER WOOKBOOK

Author's Craft Deep Dive

Find one example of strong writing (imagery, symbolism, dialogue, or structure).

The author wrote____

____

____

____

This technique is effective because ______________________

____

____

____

Critical Response

Do you agree with the author's message or perspective? Explain your thinking.

____

____

____

____

Metacognitive Reflection

What did this book help you understand better about yourself, others, or the world?

____

____

____

____

Interpret, Analyze, Argue   Book 16

Book Title: ____

Author: ____

Date:____

What Is the Author's Central Message?

Write a clear claim about what the author is trying to say about life, people, or the world

____

____

____

What Themes Appear in the Story?

List two themes and briefly explain each.

*Theme 1*____

____

Explain how this theme appears in the story _______________

____

____

____

*Theme 2*____

____

Explain how this theme appears in the story _______________

____

____

____

Character as an Idea

Choose one main character. What idea does this character represent?

____

____

____

Key Scene Analysis

Describe one scene that is especially important.

____

____

____

Why is this scene important to the story's meaning?

____

____

____

Evidence Matters

Write two pieces of evidence from the text that support your ideas.

*Evidence 1*____________________________________

____

____

*Evidence 2*____________________________________

____

____

Setting and Meaning

How does the setting influence the story's themes or conflicts?

____

____

____

____

Author's Perspective

What does the author seem to believe about people or the world?

____

____

____

____

____

Compare Texts

Think about another book you've read.

This book is similar to____________________________________

____

____

because both texts____

____

____

THE HAPPY READER WOOKBOOK

Author's Craft Deep Dive

Find one example of strong writing (imagery, symbolism, dialogue, or structure).

The author wrote____

____

____

____

This technique is effective because ____________________________

____

____

____

Critical Response

Do you agree with the author's message or perspective? Explain your thinking.

____

____

____

____

Metacognitive Reflection

What did this book help you understand better about yourself, others, or the world?

____

____

____

____

Interpret, Analyze, Argue

Book 17

Book Title: ____

Author: ____

Date:____

What Is the Author's Central Message?

Write a clear claim about what the author is trying to say about life, people, or the world

____

____

____

What Themes Appear in the Story?

List two themes and briefly explain each.

*Theme 1*_______________________________________

____

Explain how this theme appears in the story _______________

____

____

____

*Theme 2*_______________________________________

____

Explain how this theme appears in the story _______________

____

____

____

THE HAPPY READER WOOKBOOK

Character as an Idea

Choose one main character. What idea does this character represent?

____

____

____

Key Scene Analysis

Describe one scene that is especially important.

____

____

____

Why is this scene important to the story's meaning?

____

____

____

Evidence Matters

Write two pieces of evidence from the text that support your ideas.

*Evidence 1*_______________________________________

____

____

*Evidence 2*_______________________________________

____

____

Setting and Meaning

How does the setting influence the story's themes or conflicts?

____

____

____

____

Author's Perspective

What does the author seem to believe about people or the world?

____

____

____

____

____

Compare Texts

Think about another book you've read.

This book is similar to____

____

____

because both texts____

____

____

THE HAPPY READER WOOKBOOK

Author's Craft Deep Dive

Find one example of strong writing (imagery, symbolism, dialogue, or structure).

The author wrote_______________________________________

____

____

This technique is effective because __________________

____

____

____

Critical Response

Do you agree with the author's message or perspective? Explain your thinking.

____

____

____

____

Metacognitive Reflection

What did this book help you understand better about yourself, others, or the world?

____

____

____

____

Interpret, Analyze, Argue   Book 18

Book Title: ____

Author: ____

Date: ____

What Is the Author's Central Message?

Write a clear claim about what the author is trying to say about life, people, or the world

____

____

____

What Themes Appear in the Story?

List two themes and briefly explain each.

*Theme 1*_____________________________________

____

Explain how this theme appears in the story ____________

____

____

____

*Theme 2*_____________________________________

____

Explain how this theme appears in the story ____________

____

____

____

Character as an Idea

Choose one main character. What idea does this character represent?

____

____

____

Key Scene Analysis

Describe one scene that is especially important.

____

____

____

Why is this scene important to the story's meaning?

____

____

____

Evidence Matters

Write two pieces of evidence from the text that support your ideas.

*Evidence 1*____

____

____

*Evidence 2*____

____

____

Setting and Meaning

How does the setting influence the story's themes or conflicts?

____

____

____

____

Author's Perspective

What does the author seem to believe about people or the world?

____

____

____

____

Compare Texts

Think about another book you've read.

This book is similar to_________________________________

____

____

because both texts_________________________________

____

____

Author's Craft Deep Dive

Find one example of strong writing (imagery, symbolism, dialogue, or structure).

The author wrote ____

____

____

____

This technique is effective because _______________________

____

____

____

Critical Response

Do you agree with the author's message or perspective? Explain your thinking.

____

____

____

____

Metacognitive Reflection

What did this book help you understand better about yourself, others, or the world?

____

____

____

____

Interpret, Analyze, Argue   Book 19

Book Title: ____

Author: ____

Date:____

What Is the Author's Central Message?

Write a clear claim about what the author is trying to say about life, people, or the world

____

____

____

What Themes Appear in the Story?

List two themes and briefly explain each.

*Theme 1*____

____

Explain how this theme appears in the story ________________

____

____

____

*Theme 2*____

____

Explain how this theme appears in the story ________________

____

____

____

Character as an Idea

Choose one main character. What idea does this character represent?

____

____

____

Key Scene Analysis

Describe one scene that is especially important.

____

____

____

Why is this scene important to the story's meaning?

____

____

____

Evidence Matters

Write two pieces of evidence from the text that support your ideas.

*Evidence 1*____________________________________

____

____

*Evidence 2*____________________________________

____

____

Setting and Meaning

How does the setting influence the story's themes or conflicts?

____

____

____

____

Author's Perspective

What does the author seem to believe about people or the world?

____

____

____

____

____

Compare Texts

Think about another book you've read.

This book is similar to_____________________________

____

____

because both texts_________________________________

____

____

Author's Craft Deep Dive

Find one example of strong writing (imagery, symbolism, dialogue, or structure).

The author wrote____

____

____

This technique is effective because ___________________________

____

____

____

Critical Response

Do you agree with the author's message or perspective? Explain your thinking.

____

____

____

____

Metacognitive Reflection

What did this book help you understand better about yourself, others, or the world?

____

____

____

____

Interpret, Analyze, Argue   Book 20

Book Title: ____

Author: ____

Date:____

What Is the Author's Central Message?

   Write a clear claim about what the author is trying to say about life, people, or the world

____

____

____

What Themes Appear in the Story?

   List two themes and briefly explain each.

   *Theme 1*____

____

   Explain how this theme appears in the story ________________

____

____

____

   *Theme 2*____

____

   Explain how this theme appears in the story ________________

____

____

____

THE HAPPY READER WOOKBOOK

Character as an Idea

Choose one main character. What idea does this character represent?

____

____

____

Key Scene Analysis

Describe one scene that is especially important.

____

____

____

Why is this scene important to the story's meaning?

____

____

____

Evidence Matters

Write two pieces of evidence from the text that support your ideas.

*Evidence 1*_______________________________________

____

____

*Evidence 2*_______________________________________

____

____

Setting and Meaning

How does the setting influence the story's themes or conflicts?

____

____

____

____

Author's Perspective

What does the author seem to believe about people or the world?

____

____

____

____

____

Compare Texts

Think about another book you've read.

This book is similar to_______________________________

____

____

because both texts_______________________________

____

____

Author's Craft Deep Dive

Find one example of strong writing (imagery, symbolism, dialogue, or structure).

The author wrote____

____

____

____

This technique is effective because ___________________

____

____

____

Critical Response

Do you agree with the author's message or perspective? Explain your thinking.

____

____

____

____

Metacognitive Reflection

What did this book help you understand better about yourself, others, or the world?

____

____

____

____

GRADE 5

Interpret, Analyze, Argue   Book 21

Book Title: ____

Author: ____

Date:____

What Is the Author's Central Message?

Write a clear claim about what the author is trying to say about life, people, or the world

____

____

____

What Themes Appear in the Story?

List two themes and briefly explain each.

*Theme 1*____

____

Explain how this theme appears in the story _______________

____

____

____

*Theme 2*____

____

Explain how this theme appears in the story _______________

____

____

____

Character as an Idea

Choose one main character. What idea does this character represent?

____

____

____

Key Scene Analysis

Describe one scene that is especially important.

____

____

____

Why is this scene important to the story's meaning?

____

____

____

Evidence Matters

Write two pieces of evidence from the text that support your ideas.

*Evidence 1*____

____

____

____

*Evidence 2*____

____

____

____

Setting and Meaning

How does the setting influence the story's themes or conflicts?

____

____

____

____

Author's Perspective

What does the author seem to believe about people or the world?

____

____

____

____

Compare Texts

Think about another book you've read.

This book is similar to_______________________________

____

____

because both texts_______________________________

____

____

Author's Craft Deep Dive

Find one example of strong writing (imagery, symbolism, dialogue, or structure).

The author wrote____

____

____

____

This technique is effective because _______________________

____

____

____

Critical Response

Do you agree with the author's message or perspective? Explain your thinking.

____

____

____

____

Metacognitive Reflection

What did this book help you understand better about yourself, others, or the world?

____

____

____

____

Interpret, Analyze, Argue

Book 22

Book Title: ____

Author: ____

Date:____

What Is the Author's Central Message?

Write a clear claim about what the author is trying to say about life, people, or the world

____

____

____

What Themes Appear in the Story?

List two themes and briefly explain each.

*Theme 1*____

____

Explain how this theme appears in the story ______________________

____

____

____

*Theme 2*____

____

Explain how this theme appears in the story ______________________

____

____

____

Character as an Idea

Choose one main character. What idea does this character represent?

____

____

____

Key Scene Analysis

Describe one scene that is especially important.

____

____

____

Why is this scene important to the story's meaning?

____

____

____

Evidence Matters

Write two pieces of evidence from the text that support your ideas.

*Evidence 1*_______________________________________

____

____

*Evidence 2*_______________________________________

____

____

Setting and Meaning

How does the setting influence the story's themes or conflicts?

____

____

____

____

Author's Perspective

What does the author seem to believe about people or the world?

____

____

____

____

Compare Texts

Think about another book you've read.

This book is similar to_________________________

____

____

because both texts_____________________________

____

____

Author's Craft Deep Dive

Find one example of strong writing (imagery, symbolism, dialogue, or structure).

The author wrote____

____

____

This technique is effective because __________________________

____

____

____

Critical Response

Do you agree with the author's message or perspective? Explain your thinking.

____

____

____

____

Metacognitive Reflection

What did this book help you understand better about yourself, others, or the world?

____

____

____

____

Interpret, Analyze, Argue   Book 23

Book Title: ____

Author: ____

Date: ____

What Is the Author's Central Message?

Write a clear claim about what the author is trying to say about life, people, or the world

____

____

____

What Themes Appear in the Story?

List two themes and briefly explain each.

Theme 1 ____

____

Explain how this theme appears in the story _____________________

____

____

____

Theme 2 ____

____

Explain how this theme appears in the story _____________________

____

____

____

Character as an Idea

Choose one main character. What idea does this character represent?

____

____

____

Key Scene Analysis

Describe one scene that is especially important.

____

____

____

Why is this scene important to the story's meaning?

____

____

____

Evidence Matters

Write two pieces of evidence from the text that support your ideas.

*Evidence 1*_______________________________________

____

____

*Evidence 2*_______________________________________

____

____

Setting and Meaning

How does the setting influence the story's themes or conflicts?

____

____

____

____

Author's Perspective

What does the author seem to believe about people or the world?

____

____

____

____

Compare Texts

Think about another book you've read.

This book is similar to______________________________

____

____

because both texts______________________________

____

____

Author's Craft Deep Dive

Find one example of strong writing (imagery, symbolism, dialogue, or structure).

The author wrote____

____

____

____

This technique is effective because ____________________________

____

____

____

Critical Response

Do you agree with the author's message or perspective? Explain your thinking.

____

____

____

____

Metacognitive Reflection

What did this book help you understand better about yourself, others, or the world?

____

____

____

____

Interpret, Analyze, Argue   Book 24

Book Title: ____

Author: ____

Date:____

What Is the Author's Central Message?

Write a clear claim about what the author is trying to say about life, people, or the world

____

____

____

What Themes Appear in the Story?

List two themes and briefly explain each.

*Theme 1*______________________________________

____

Explain how this theme appears in the story ___________

____

____

____

*Theme 2*______________________________________

____

Explain how this theme appears in the story ___________

____

____

____

Character as an Idea

Choose one main character. What idea does this character represent?

____

____

____

Key Scene Analysis

Describe one scene that is especially important.

____

____

____

Why is this scene important to the story's meaning?

____

____

____

Evidence Matters

Write two pieces of evidence from the text that support your ideas.

*Evidence 1*_________________________________

____

____

*Evidence 2*_________________________________

____

____

Setting and Meaning

How does the setting influence the story's themes or conflicts?

____

____

____

____

Author's Perspective

What does the author seem to believe about people or the world?

____

____

____

____

Compare Texts

Think about another book you've read.

This book is similar to_______________________________

____

____

because both texts_______________________________

____

____

Author's Craft Deep Dive

Find one example of strong writing (imagery, symbolism, dialogue, or structure).

The author wrote____

____

____

____

This technique is effective because _______________________________

____

____

____

Critical Response

Do you agree with the author's message or perspective? Explain your thinking.

____

____

____

____

Metacognitive Reflection

What did this book help you understand better about yourself, others, or the world?

____

____

____

____

Interpret, Analyze, Argue   Book 25

Book Title: ____

Author: ____

Date: ____

What Is the Author's Central Message?

Write a clear claim about what the author is trying to say about life, people, or the world

____

____

____

What Themes Appear in the Story?

List two themes and briefly explain each.

Theme 1 ____

____

Explain how this theme appears in the story __________________

____

____

____

Theme 2 ____

____

Explain how this theme appears in the story __________________

____

____

____

THE HAPPY READER WOOKBOOK

Character as an Idea

Choose one main character. What idea does this character represent?

____

____

____

Key Scene Analysis

Describe one scene that is especially important.

____

____

____

Why is this scene important to the story's meaning?

____

____

____

Evidence Matters

Write two pieces of evidence from the text that support your ideas.

*Evidence 1*___________________________________

____

____

*Evidence 2*___________________________________

____

____

Setting and Meaning

How does the setting influence the story's themes or conflicts?

____

____

____

____

Author's Perspective

What does the author seem to believe about people or the world?

____

____

____

____

____

Compare Texts

Think about another book you've read.

This book is similar to_______________________________

____

____

because both texts_______________________________

____

____

Author's Craft Deep Dive

Find one example of strong writing (imagery, symbolism, dialogue, or structure).

The author wrote____

____

____

This technique is effective because ___________________

____

____

____

Critical Response

Do you agree with the author's message or perspective? Explain your thinking.

____

____

____

____

Metacognitive Reflection

What did this book help you understand better about yourself, others, or the world?

____

____

____

____

GRADE 5

Interpret, Analyze, Argue

Book 26

Book Title: ____

Author: ____

Date:____

What Is the Author's Central Message?

Write a clear claim about what the author is trying to say about life, people, or the world

____

____

____

What Themes Appear in the Story?

List two themes and briefly explain each.

*Theme 1*____

____

Explain how this theme appears in the story ___________________

____

____

____

*Theme 2*____

____

Explain how this theme appears in the story ___________________

____

____

____

Character as an Idea

Choose one main character. What idea does this character represent?

____

____

____

Key Scene Analysis

Describe one scene that is especially important.

____

____

____

Why is this scene important to the story's meaning?

____

____

____

Evidence Matters

Write two pieces of evidence from the text that support your ideas.

*Evidence 1*______________________________________

____

____

*Evidence 2*______________________________________

____

____

Setting and Meaning

How does the setting influence the story's themes or conflicts?

____

____

____

____

Author's Perspective

What does the author seem to believe about people or the world?

____

____

____

____

____

Compare Texts

Think about another book you've read.

This book is similar to_______________________________

____

____

because both texts_____________________________

____

____

Author's Craft Deep Dive

Find one example of strong writing (imagery, symbolism, dialogue, or structure).

The author wrote_______________________________________

____

____

____

This technique is effective because __________________

____

____

____

Critical Response

Do you agree with the author's message or perspective? Explain your thinking.

____

____

____

____

Metacognitive Reflection

What did this book help you understand better about yourself, others, or the world?

____

____

____

____

Interpret, Analyze, Argue

Book Title: _______________________________

Author: _______________________________

Date:_______________________________

What Is the Author's Central Message?

Write a clear claim about what the author is trying to say about life, people, or the world

____

____

____

What Themes Appear in the Story?

List two themes and briefly explain each.

*Theme 1*_______________________________

____

Explain how this theme appears in the story _______________________________

____

____

____

*Theme 2*_______________________________

____

Explain how this theme appears in the story _______________________________

____

____

____

Character as an Idea

Choose one main character. What idea does this character represent?

____

____

____

Key Scene Analysis

Describe one scene that is especially important.

____

____

____

Why is this scene important to the story's meaning?

____

____

____

Evidence Matters

Write two pieces of evidence from the text that support your ideas.

*Evidence 1*_______________________________________

____

____

*Evidence 2*_______________________________________

____

____

GRADE 5

Setting and Meaning

How does the setting influence the story's themes or conflicts?

____

____

____

____

Author's Perspective

What does the author seem to believe about people or the world?

____

____

____

____

Compare Texts

Think about another book you've read.

This book is similar to_________________________________

____

____

because both texts____________________________________

____

____

Author's Craft Deep Dive

Find one example of strong writing (imagery, symbolism, dialogue, or structure).

The author wrote___________________________________

____

____

____

This technique is effective because ___________________

____

____

____

Critical Response

Do you agree with the author's message or perspective? Explain your thinking.

____

____

____

____

Metacognitive Reflection

What did this book help you understand better about yourself, others, or the world?

____

____

____

____

Interpret, Analyze, Argue

Book 28

Book Title: ____

Author: ____

Date:____

What Is the Author's Central Message?

Write a clear claim about what the author is trying to say about life, people, or the world

____

____

____

What Themes Appear in the Story?

List two themes and briefly explain each.

*Theme 1*_______________________________________

____

Explain how this theme appears in the story _______________

____

____

____

*Theme 2*_______________________________________

____

Explain how this theme appears in the story _______________

____

____

____

Character as an Idea

Choose one main character. What idea does this character represent?

____

____

____

Key Scene Analysis

Describe one scene that is especially important.

____

____

____

Why is this scene important to the story's meaning?

____

____

____

Evidence Matters

Write two pieces of evidence from the text that support your ideas.

*Evidence 1*_______________________________________

____

____

*Evidence 2*_______________________________________

____

____

Setting and Meaning

How does the setting influence the story's themes or conflicts?

____

____

____

____

Author's Perspective

What does the author seem to believe about people or the world?

____

____

____

____

Compare Texts

Think about another book you've read.

This book is similar to_______________________

____

____

because both texts_______________________

____

____

Author's Craft Deep Dive

Find one example of strong writing (imagery, symbolism, dialogue, or structure).

The author wrote____

____

____

This technique is effective because _______________________

____

____

____

Critical Response

Do you agree with the author's message or perspective? Explain your thinking.

____

____

____

____

Metacognitive Reflection

What did this book help you understand better about yourself, others, or the world?

____

____

____

____

Interpret, Analyze, Argue   Book 29

Book Title: ____

Author: ____

Date:____

What Is the Author's Central Message?

Write a clear claim about what the author is trying to say about life, people, or the world

____

____

____

What Themes Appear in the Story?

List two themes and briefly explain each.

*Theme 1*____

____

Explain how this theme appears in the story _______________

____

____

____

*Theme 2*____

____

Explain how this theme appears in the story _______________

____

____

____

Character as an Idea

Choose one main character. What idea does this character represent?

____

____

____

Key Scene Analysis

Describe one scene that is especially important.

____

____

____

Why is this scene important to the story's meaning?

____

____

____

Evidence Matters

Write two pieces of evidence from the text that support your ideas.

*Evidence 1*_______________________________________

____

____

____

*Evidence 2*_______________________________________

____

____

____

Setting and Meaning

How does the setting influence the story's themes or conflicts?

____

____

____

____

Author's Perspective

What does the author seem to believe about people or the world?

____

____

____

____

____

Compare Texts

Think about another book you've read.

This book is similar to_______________________________

____

____

because both texts_______________________________

____

____

Author's Craft Deep Dive

Find one example of strong writing (imagery, symbolism, dialogue, or structure).

The author wrote____

____

____

____

This technique is effective because _____________________________

____

____

____

Critical Response

Do you agree with the author's message or perspective? Explain your thinking.

____

____

____

____

Metacognitive Reflection

What did this book help you understand better about yourself, others, or the world?

____

____

____

____

Interpret, Analyze, Argue   Book 30

Book Title: ____

Author: ____

Date:____

What Is the Author's Central Message?

Write a clear claim about what the author is trying to say about life, people, or the world

____

____

____

What Themes Appear in the Story?

List two themes and briefly explain each.

*Theme 1*____

____

Explain how this theme appears in the story ______________________

____

____

____

*Theme 2*____

____

Explain how this theme appears in the story ______________________

____

____

____

THE HAPPY READER WOOKBOOK

Character as an Idea

Choose one main character. What idea does this character represent?

____

____

____

Key Scene Analysis

Describe one scene that is especially important.

____

____

____

Why is this scene important to the story's meaning?

____

____

____

Evidence Matters

Write two pieces of evidence from the text that support your ideas.

*Evidence 1*_______________________________________

____

____

*Evidence 2*_______________________________________

____

____

Setting and Meaning

How does the setting influence the story's themes or conflicts?

____

____

____

____

Author's Perspective

What does the author seem to believe about people or the world?

____

____

____

____

____

Compare Texts

Think about another book you've read.

This book is similar to_______________________________

____

____

because both texts_______________________________

____

____

THE HAPPY READER WOOKBOOK

Author's Craft Deep Dive

Find one example of strong writing (imagery, symbolism, dialogue, or structure).

The author wrote____

____

____

This technique is effective because ___________________________

____

____

____

Critical Response

Do you agree with the author's message or perspective? Explain your thinking.

____

____

____

____

Metacognitive Reflection

What did this book help you understand better about yourself, others, or the world?

____

____

____

____

My Reading List

1. ____

2. ____

3. ____

4. ____

5. ____

6. ____

7. ____

8. ____

9. ____

10. ____

11. ____

12. ____

13. ____

14. ____

15. ____

My Reading List

16. ____

17. ____

18. ____

19. ____

20. ____

21. ____

22. ____

23. ____

24. ____

25. ____

26. ____

27. ____

28. ____

29. ____

30. ____

GRADE 5

Reader's Post-Reading Self-Assessment

Please choose how you feel about each sentence. Circle one.

1.   I evaluate characters, ideas, or choices.

        Always (5)   Often (4)   Sometimes (3)   Rarely (2)   Not yet (1)

2.   I use evidence to support my ideas.

        Always (5)   Often (4)   Sometimes (3)   Rarely (2)   Not yet (1)

3.   I reflect on how reading shapes my thinking.

        Always (5)   Often (4)   Sometimes (3)   Rarely (2)   Not yet (1)

4.   I read with purpose and independence.

        Always (5)   Often (4)   Sometimes (3)   Rarely (2)   Not yet (1)

5.   I look for patterns across a text.

        Always (5)   Often (4)   Sometimes (3)   Rarely (2)   Not yet (1)

Total score (optional): ____ / 25

How do I connect the ideas or themes in a story with other stories I've read, or to my own thoughts?

____

____

____

____

____

THE HAPPY READER WOOKBOOK

Post-Reading Assessment by Parent, Caregiver, Teacher, or Helper

Adult Observation Inventory: Rate your observations of the reader.

1.   Looks past the literal meaning in the text

        Consistently (5)   Often (4)   Sometimes (3)   Rarely (2)   Not observed (1)

2.   Uses evidence or examples for statements

        Consistently (5)   Often (4)   Sometimes (3)   Rarely (2)   Not observed (1)

3.   Searches for patterns in characters' behavior or story themes

        Consistently (5)   Often (4)   Sometimes (3)   Rarely (2)   Not observed (1)

4.   Demonstrates sustained engagement in the understanding of the text

        Consistently (5)   Often (4)   Sometimes (3)   Rarely (2)   Not observed (1)

5.   Demonstrates sustained engagement in the interpretation of the text

        Consistently (5)   Often (4)   Sometimes (3)   Rarely (2)   Not observed (1)

Total score (optional): ____ / 25

Qualitative assessment:

How does my child compare ideas or themes across different texts?________________
____
____

How does my child evaluate author assumptions or arguments?________________
____
____

How do I encourage critical thinking, reflection, and textual argumentation?____________
____
____

GRADE 5

Understanding Your Child's Post-Reading Assessment

Grade 5 readers synthesize ideas, evaluate perspectives, and read with intention. This assessment reflects readiness for advanced literacy demands.

What This Assessment Measures

The questions examine whether your child:
- Integrates ideas across a text
- Evaluates arguments or messages
- Uses evidence strategically
- Reflects on how reading shapes thinking

These skills signal mature comprehension.

Why These Skills Matter

Revised Bloom's Taxonomy explains how higher-level thinking moves from understanding toward evaluation and creation. *Disciplinary Literacy* research shows that advanced readers think critically about how texts work and why ideas are presented in certain ways. *Self-Determination Theory* highlights the importance of autonomy and purpose in sustained reading engagement.

How to Use the Assessment

Look for consistency across different types of texts. Higher scores suggest strong preparedness for middle-grade literacy. Moderate scores suggest reasoning that benefits from conversation. Lower scores may indicate difficulty in certain areas that require expert evaluation.

What to Do Next

Encourage comparison across texts. Invite thoughtful disagreement. Discuss how reading informs views of the world. Independent readers think critically and responsibly.

THE HAPPY READER WOOKBOOK

A Final Word to Parents, Caregivers, Teachers, and Helpers

Congratulations! Your child has completed the pre- and post-reading assessments for Grade 5. He or she has developed skills in synthesis, evaluation, and evidence-based argumentation.

- Your child can now identify themes, evaluate author assumptions, and compare texts thoughtfully.
- You have fostered independent reasoning and discussion, supporting Critical Literacy, Gradual Release of Responsibility, and Evidence-Based Thinking.

Everyday Ways to Encourage Growth

- Encourage discussion of themes, assumptions, and textual connections in books, articles, or everyday media.
- Ask him or her to support opinions with multiple pieces of evidence in conversation or writing.
- Encourage reflective writing or journaling about ideas in the world and in stories.

Looking Ahead

Your child will transition to middle school next year. Skills in critical thinking, synthesis, and evidence-based reasoning will support success across subjects. Your ongoing support in discussion, reflection, and reading independence is crucial for continued growth.

Explore More Resources

Visit www.starryfieldpress.com for additional resources through our our children's imprint, Via Risus. Join our email list to receive updates, enrichment ideas, and reading support strategies. You may scan the QR code below:

STARRY FIELD PRESS

Glossary

Author's Craft

Author's craft refers to deliberate choices in language, structure, tone, and symbolism. Readers analyze how these choices shape meaning. Craft moves beyond content.

Why this matters

Understanding craft deepens comprehension.

Everyday use

Ask why the author wrote something a certain way.

Authorial Assumptions

Authorial assumptions are beliefs an author takes for granted. Readers identify implicit viewpoints. This supports critique.

Why this matters

Recognizing assumptions strengthens analysis.

Everyday use

Ask what the author assumes the reader believes.

Bloom's Revised Taxonomy

Bloom's Revised Taxonomy describes levels of thinking from remembering to creating. Upper grades emphasize analysis, evaluation, and synthesis. This frame work guides questioning.

Why this matters

It supports higher-order thinking.

Everyday use

Encourage explaining and evaluating ideas.

Critical Literacy

Critical literacy involves examining texts for assumptions, perspectives, and power relationships. Readers consider whose voices are present or absent. This fosters independence.

Why this matters

Critical literacy promotes thoughtful reading.

Everyday use

Discuss whose perspective is shown.

THE HAPPY READER WOOKBOOK

Glossary

Perspective Analysis

Perspective analysis examines how point of view shapes meaning. Readers consider bias and reliability. Perspective influences interpretation.

Why this matters

Perspective analysis supports critical thinking.

Everyday use

Discuss how another narrator might tell the story.

Textual Argumentation

Textual argumentation involves making claims supported by evidence. Readers jus tify interpretations logically. This skill supports academic writing.

Why this matters

Argumentation prepares students for formal discourse.

Everyday use

Ask for opinions supported by reasons.

Transfer of Learning

Transfer of learning involves applying skills across contexts. Readers use strategies flexibly. Transfer indicates deep understanding.

Why this matters

Transfer shows mastery.

Everyday use

Ask how a strategy worked in a new text.

Selected References

Afflerbach, P., Pearson, P. D., & Paris, S. G. (2008). Clarifying differences between reading skills and reading strategies. *The Reading Teacher, 61*(5), 364–373.

Graesser, A. C., Singer, M., & Trabasso, T. (1994). Constructing inferences during narrative text comprehension. *Psychological Review, 101*(3), 371–395.

Graham, S. (2020). The sciences of reading and writing must become more fully integrated. *Reading Research Quarterly, 55*(S1), S35–S44.

McNamara, D. S., & Magliano, J. (2009). Toward a comprehensive model of comprehension. *Psychology of Learning and Motivation, 51*, 297–384.

Shanahan, T., & Shanahan, C. (2008). Teaching disciplinary literacy to adolescents. *Harvard Educational Review, 78*(1), 40–59.

Snow, C. E., & Moje, E. B. (2010). Is literacy enough? *Journal of Literacy Research, 42*(3), 301–317.

More from *The Happy Reader* Series

Reading Comprehension Workbook, Grade K – Meaning & Story Sense
- Identify characters and settings
- Retell events orally and visually
- Express feelings and preferences
- Develop narrative awareness

Reading Comprehension Workbook, Grade 1 – Story Structure & Explanation
- Identify problem and solution
- Beginning–middle–end sequencing
- Simple cause-and-effect
- Introduce written responses
- Early moral and lesson identification

Reading Comprehension Workbook, Grade 2 – Cause, Change, and Evidence
- Character motivation
- Explicit cause–effect reasoning
- Textual clues for feelings
- Vocabulary in context
- "Because…" reasoning

Reading Comprehension Workbook, Grade 3 – Inference & Theme
- Main idea vs. details
- Theme identification and defense
- Evidence-based explanations
- Paragraph-level summaries
- Metacognitive reflection

Reading Comprehension Workbook, Grade 4 – Analysis & Perspective
- Theme as an argument
- Character development arcs
- Point of view and symbolism
- Paragraph writing with evidence
- Author's craft analysis

Reading Comprehension Workbook, Grade 5 – Synthesis & Argument
- Author's message and assumptions
- Multiple themes
- Text-to-text comparison
- Literary critique
- Reflective and analytical writing

GRADE 5